Barbie™

Dress up

ULTIMATE STICKER COLLECTION

How to use this book

Read the captions, then find the sticker that best fits the space.
(Hint: check the bold sticker labels for clues!)

•

There are lots of fantastic extra stickers for creating
your own scenes throughout the book.

DK | Penguin Random House

Written by Laura Gilbert
Project editor Lisa Stock
Designer Elena Jarmoskaite
Project art editor Jenny Edwards

This American Edition, 2023
Published in the United States by DK Publishing
1745 Broadway, 20th Floor, New York, NY 10019

Page design copyright © 2023 Dorling Kindersley Limited
DK, a Division of Penguin Random House LLC
24 25 26 10 9 8 7 6
008–335920–06/2023

A catalog record for this book is available from
the Library of Congress.

ISBN: 978-0-7440-8278-4

DK books are available at special discounts when
purchased in bulk for sales promotions, premiums,
fund-raising, or educational use. For details, contact:
DK Publishing Special Markets,
1745 Broadway, 20th Floor, New York, NY 10019
SpecialSales@dk.com

Printed and bound in China

www.mattel.com

For the curious

www.dk.com

Follow your dreams

Barbie knows that she can do anything she wants to do, whether it's striding down the runway or caring for dogs. What do you love to do the most?

Headset

Protective helmet

Pink guitar

Suit with reflective strips

Rock star

Imagine performing in front of thousands of people! You'll need a headset, an instrument, and an outfit to match your music.

Fighting fire

A firefighter's uniform protects them against fire and is easy to put on. They need to be ready in an instant!

High-top sneakers

Visor

Metallic
jacket

Animal lover
Dog trainers have to be
as active as their canine
companions. Sneakers
and shorts are a must.

Breathable
top

Sparkly dog
collar

Clutch
purse

Lightweight
shorts

Fashion icon
Some people like to
express themselves
through fashion. Metallic
mauve and pink make a
cool statement!

Yellow
sneakers

3

Basketball jersey

Shooting hoops

This basketball player is about to shoot. Long shorts and a long-length top help her stretch up easily.

Headband

Tank top

Navy-and-white shorts

Tennis racket

Pink-trimmed tennis skirt

Ace it

A tennis player runs around the court a lot, so they need comfortable clothing. A headband keeps their hair out of their eyes.

Pink sneakers

Getting sporty

Sports can be played as part of a team, against one player, or even on your own. Whatever the sport, make sure you have the right gear!

Blue helmet

Red tank top

Top of the world

Rock climbers use a harness and special clips called carabiners. The view at the top makes the climb worth it!

Black belt

Striped top

Wide-legged pants

Denim shorts

Orange boots

Strength and discipline

The belt that a martial artist wears shows how skilled they are. The highest level belt is a black belt.

Backpack with water and snacks

Giddy-up!

In horseback riding, the rider and the horse both wear special equipment. A blanket under the saddle protects the horse and the rider wears a helmet.

Bodywarmer

Pink helmet

Saddle

Crop top

Padded gloves

Long shorts

In the ring

Boxing is a combat sport. Boxers wear special gloves, and boots that support their ankles as they bounce around the ring.

Pink boots

Ready, steady, go!

Barbie loves to be active. She doesn't mind if it's at the pool, at the skate park, or on the balance beam. What's your favorite sport?

Neat hairstyle

Goggles

Patterned leotard

Keep your balance

Gymnasts wear flexible leotards so they can leap and tumble on the floor with ease.

Gymnastic ribbon

Swimsuit

Making a splash

This swimmer has just won a gold medal. All the hours of practice were worth it for this incredible moment!

Stickers for pages 2-3

Protective helmet

Breathable top

Yellow sneakers

Sparkly dog collar

Suit with reflective strips

Lightweight shorts

Visor

Headset

YOU CAN BE AN ASTRONAUT
Barbie
STAMP OF EXCELLENCE

Clutch purse

High-top sneakers

Pink guitar

Metallic jacket

Chicken

Brown hat

Stethoscope

Logo t-shirt

Pink shirt

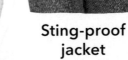

Waterproof tall boots

Puppy

Blue shorts

Khaki shorts

Hat and protective veil

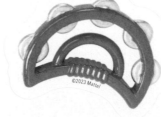

Sting-proof jacket

Cream-colored boots

Yellow chick

Jeans

Sturdy brown shoes

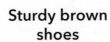

Koala

Stickers for pages 6-7

Red hairband

Mixing bowl

Double-breasted red jacket

Chef's hat

Apron

Frying pan

Mixing spoon

White sneakers

Pinstripe pants

EPIC CHEF IN TRAINING

Barbie

Pink shoes

Pockets for utensils

Noodle logo t-shirt

Denim skirt

©2023 Mattel

Stickers for pages 8-9

Violin bow

Tiara

Violin

Sparkly pink bodice

Soft pink tights

Loose top

Classical short tutu

Patterned leggings

Metallic skirt

Microphone

Turquoise shoes

Cropped leggings

Strappy sandals

Microphone stand

©2023 Mattel

Stickers for pages 10–11

Black lace-up shoes

Robot

Stethoscope

Mid-sleeved lab coat

Lab coat

Black jeans

New toothbrush

Teal-colored scrubs

Heeled black shoes

Lightweight jacket

White sneakers

©2023 Mattel

Stickers for pages 12-13

Lightweight suit

Flippers

Pocketed vest

Snorkel and mask

Light khaki shorts

Protective gloves

Hat with headlight

Camera

Waterproof shorts

Tan boots

Pilot's hat

Pants with blue detailing

Double-breasted blue jacket

Navy pants

Stickers for pages 14-15

Comfy sneakers

Paint palette

Casual jeans

Steel-toe boots

High-visibility vest

Judge's robe

Formal black shoes

Khaki jacket

Hard-wearing denim jeans

Protective hard hat

Painter's apron

Black pants

White sneakers

Design in progress

©2023 Mattel

Stickers for pages 16–17

White helmet

Pink-trimmed tennis skirt

Tank top

Tennis racket

Warm jersey

Soccer jersey

Basketball jersey

Red pants

Ice skates

Shin guards

Pink sneakers

Navy-and-white shorts

Soccer ball

Soccer shorts

Puck